After Kyoto: Are There Rational Pathways to a Sustainable Global Energy System?

1998 Aspen Energy Policy Forum
Roger W. Sant, Chairman

Paul Runci, Rapporteur
John A. Riggs, Program Director

For additional copies of this paper, please contact:

The Aspen Institute
Publications Office
109 Houghton Lab Lane
P.O. Box 222
Queenstown, MD 21658
Phone: (410) 820-5338
Fax: (410) 827-9174
E-mail: publications@aspeninst.org

For all other inquiries, please contact:

The Aspen Institute
Program on Energy, the Environment, and the Economy
Suite 1070
1333 New Hampshire Avenue, NW
Washington, DC 20036
Phone: (202) 736-5823
Fax: (202) 293-0525

ISBN:0-89843-251-0

Table of Contents

Foreword   1

Forum Agenda   5

Summary and Conclusions   9

Session I: International Perspectives on the Kyoto Agreement   15

Session II: Governance and Policy Instruments   23

Session III: Economics   29

Session IV: Technology   33

List of Participants   39

The Aspen Institute Program on Energy, the Environment,
and the Economy   49

AFTER KYOTO: ARE THERE RATIONAL PATHWAYS
TO A SUSTAINABLE GLOBAL ENERGY SYSTEM?

1

Foreword

Each year since 1977 the Aspen Institute has convened a group of energy leaders from diverse backgrounds in its Energy Policy Forum to discuss a timely topic of importance to the energy world. The goal of the Forum, as with all Institute policy programs, is to improve the quality of leadership and policy formulation. The atmosphere is designed to foster the free exchange of opinions and information and to encourage creative thinking.

Interaction among business leaders, economists, lawyers, scientists, engineers, and politicians ensures that an issue is examined from the perspective of various disciplines. Representation from industry, environmental groups, government, academia, and, increasingly, other countries brings various values and viewpoints to bear.

Following the December, 1997, Kyoto Agreement on climate change, the 1998 Forum took as its topic *After Kyoto: Are There Rational Pathways to a Sustainable Global System?"* The intensity of the political debate over ratification and the agreement's potentially far-reaching implications for the energy industry made the issue an obvious choice. The Forum chose to look at achieving long-term sustainability as well as the desirability and feasibility of compliance with the near-term emissions reduction goals of the Agreement. An initial understanding that participants would not debate the science of climate change helped reduce the decibels, increase the lumens, and allow the discovery of areas of common ground. As this report indicates, those areas were substantial.

In many ways this was an ideal topic for an Aspen Energy Policy Forum. It involved basic questions of values, including economic growth and the environment, international and intergenerational equity, and distribution of wealth. It involved questions of policy, including how national governments can implement an international policy, and how the political world will balance an equation in which not only the costs and benefits are uncertain, but also the distribution of those costs and benefits—regionally, sectorally, and temporally. The topic also was ideally suited to the Forum's multi-disciplinary approach: the interrelated issues involve economics, science and technology, domestic and international governance, the law, and politics.

Given the broad differences of opinion that characterize this issue, the group was pleasantly surprised at how much agreement emerged during the dialogue. People who disagreed on the merits of the Kyoto Agreement found themselves in agreement on longer term objectives and on near term actions to make them possible. A set of conclusions growing out of these broad areas of agreement are contained in the Summary and Conclusions section of this report and have been sent separately to the President and the Congressional leadership.

As Chair of this year's Forum, the Institute was fortunate to have Roger Sant, Chairman of the Board of the AES Corporation and of the World Wildlife Fund. His broad experience in the energy industry and his commitment to environmental issues give him an ideal background for framing and exploring an issue that so directly links these two fields.

Although lively dialogue rather than didactic presentations is the rule at the Forum, the content of each session is enriched by the initial brief presentations of experts and practitioners who help define the issues. The Forum was privileged this year to have an exceptionally talented group who enlightened, provoked, entertained, and challenged the participants.

Paul Runci of Battelle, Pacific Northwest National Laboratories again served as rapporteur, tirelessly capturing the wide-ranging views of the participants and skillfully condensing them into a comprehensible whole.

The Aspen Institute gratefully acknowledges the important role of our sponsors, whose support sustains the Program financially while also confirming our vision and affirming the value of our work.

AFTER KYOTO: ARE THERE RATIONAL PATHWAYS
TO A SUSTAINABLE GLOBAL ENERGY SYSTEM?

3

Contributions were received from the following during the past year:

ABB Power Plant Systems
American Petroleum Institute
Amoco Foundation, Inc.
Booz•Allen & Hamilton, Inc.
Cinergy Services, Inc.
Consumers Energy
Edison International
Electric Power Research
    Institute
Energy Asset Management,
    L.L.C.
Enron Corporation
William and Julie Fulkerson
Gas Research Institute
GPU Service, Inc.
Japan National Oil
    Corporation

Mitchell Energy &
    Development Corporation
Orange & Rockland Utilities
Pacific Enterprises
Paul Dragoumis Associates,
    Inc.
Potomac Electric Power
    Company
Putnam, Hayes & Bartlett
Ruhrgas, A.G.
Saudi Arabian Oil Company
Southern Company Services,
    Inc.
Summit Foundation
Trigen Energy Corporation
Verner, Liipfert, Bernhard,
    McPherson, and Hand

Finally, although this report is an attempt to represent the views expressed during the Forum, it is not a consensus document. All participants were not asked to agree to the text of the report or the wording of the conclusions. The report is issued under the authority of the Aspen Institute, and neither the Forum speakers, participants, or sponsors are responsible for its contents.

John A. Riggs
Director
Program on Energy, the Environment,
    and the Economy

AFTER KYOTO: ARE THERE RATIONAL PATHWAYS
TO A SUSTAINABLE GLOBAL ENERGY SYSTEM?

5

Forum Agenda

1998 Aspen Energy Policy Forum
**"After Kyoto: Are There Rational Pathways
to a Sustainable Global Energy System?"**

Chairman
Roger Sant
Chairman
AES Corporation

The potential policies for addressing carbon emissions are largely energy policies, so the Kyoto Agreement and other potential policies for achieving sustainability pose an interesting series of issues for the Aspen Energy Policy Forum. The far-reaching agreement may affect and be affected by technology development, changing market structures, fuel choices, economic growth and competition, and governance, suggesting that a multidisciplinary dialogue may offer valuable insights to policy makers.

Session I:
International Perspectives   Sunday, July 5, 8:30 am - 12:00
on the Kyoto Agreement

     Chair: **Jonathan Lash**
               President, World Resources Institute

    Takayuki Kimura, Ambassador for International Economic Affairs
       and Global Environmental Affairs, "The Japanese Perspective"
    Liu Zhaodong, Minister-Counsellor, Embassy of the People's
       Republic of China in the U.S., "A Developing Country
       Perspective"
    Michael Jefferson, Deputy Secretary General, World Energy
       Council, "An EU Perspective"
    Kathleen A. McGinty, Chair, Council on Environmental Quality,
       "The U.S. Perspective"

Session II:
Governance and Policy   Monday, July 6, 8:30 am - 12:00
Instruments

    Should each country choose its own reduction method? If adopted,
how could a world-wide emissions control program be implemented
and enforced? What are the implications for sovereignty? What are the
relative merits of a cap-and-trade method as opposed to energy or carbon taxes? Are the likely implementing mechanisms in the U.S. politi-
cally feasible? Can developing countries be persuaded to participate?

     Chair: **Charles B. Curtis**
               Hogan & Hartson

    Robert Stavins, Professor, Harvard University, "How Can National
       Governments Address a Global Problem?"
    David Garman, Chief of Staff, Senator Frank Murkowski,
       Chairman, Energy and Natural Resources Committee
    Dirk Forrister, Chair, White House Climate Change Task Force

     Respondent: **Philip R. Sharp,** Lecturer in Public Policy,
                        Harvard University, and former Chairman,
                        House Energy and Power Subcommittee

AFTER KYOTO: ARE THERE RATIONAL PATHWAYS
TO A SUSTAINABLE GLOBAL ENERGY SYSTEM?

7

Session III:
Economics   Monday, July 6, 2:00 - 5:30 pm

What would be the economic impacts of compliance with the Kyoto agreement or other potential carbon reduction plans? What would be the costs, based on what assumptions? How would various industries or companies respond?

Chair: **William W. Hogan**
Professor, John F. Kennedy School, Harvard

Jeff Frankel, Member, Council of Economic Advisors, "Economic Climate Change Models and the Assumptions that Drive Them"

Nebojsa Nakicenovic, Director, Environmentally Compatible Energy Project, International Institute for Applied Systems Analysis (IIASA), "Global Energy Perspectives to 2050 andBeyond"

James E. Rogers, Jr., CEO, Cinergy Corporation, "How a Coal-based Utility Will Cope"

Thomas Casten, CEO, Trigen Corporation, "Barriers to Conversion Efficiency"

Session IV:
Technology   Tuesday July 7, 8:30 am - 12:30

Can technological advances contribute to achieving the goals of the Kyoto agreement? To what extent will market forces result in adequate technological change, and to what extent will market failures require intervention by governments? How does the time frame of the goals affect the answer?

Chair: **John Bryson**
Chief Exectuive Officer, Edison International

Professor John Holdren, Chair, President's Commission on Science and Technology

Adm. Richard Truly, Director, National Renewable Energy Laboratory, "Global Opportunities for Renewable Energy"

Amory Lovins, Rocky Mountain Institute, "Putting Central Thermal Plants Out of Business"

Robert W. Shaw, Jr. , CEO, Aretê Corporation, "A Venture Capitalist Looks at Green Technologies"

Session V:
Lessons Learned   Wednesday July 8, 8:30 am - 12:00

Prefaced by a retrospective Tuesday morning from a Forum veteran on how previous Forums extracted policy lessons from dialogues, the group will split into three breakout groups for the first half of this session to determine whether guidance for policy-makers can be derived from the presentations and discussions of economics, technology, and governance. The three groups will report their conclusions back to the plenary during the second half of the session.

Chair: **Eric Zausner**
            President, Energy Asset Management

Group Moderators
  Governance: **Clinton A. Vince**
              Verner, Liipfert, Bernhard, McPherson & Hand
  Economics: **Jan Mares**
              EOP Group
  Technology: **Sheila S. Hollis**
              Duane, Morris and Heckscher

AFTER KYOTO: ARE THERE RATIONAL PATHWAYS
TO A SUSTAINABLE GLOBAL ENERGY SYSTEM?

9

Summary and Conclusions

The 1998 Energy Policy Forum addressed a number of major energy questions and challenges surrounding the Kyoto Protocol and the broader issue of how to achieve a sustainable global energy system. Since the Kyoto Protocol has sparked spirited debates over important issues such as costs of compliance, international and intergenerational equity, national sovereignty, the appropriate roles of states and markets, environmental sustainability, and the relationship of energy policy to each of these concerns, the Protocol and its context were an obvious choice of topic for this year's Forum.

In their discussions of pathways to a sustainable future energy system, Forum participants were asked by the Chair to accept two guidelines: first, to forego debate concerning the state of the science of climate change, and second, not to be limited to a discussion of near-term emissions reductions and the Kyoto Protocol. They were further asked to consider five questions or clusters of questions during their discussions:

1. Time frame.

Is climate change a problem that we need to tackle in the next 10-12 years? More specifically, should we be trying to reduce emissions now? Or should we be preparing for more drastic and perhaps more efficient reductions in the future? Should our target be an acceptable ultimate level of CO_2 concentrations, or near-term annual emissions reductions, or both?

2. Cost.

Much of the debate about ratifying the Kyoto Agreement, at least in the U.S., has revolved around the cost of compliance. Various economists derive vastly different estimates from their models, and just a few assumptions seem to be responsible for most of the differences. Is it possible to narrow the disagreements over the estimates by narrowing the disagreements on the assumptions? Examples are the extent to which fuel, technology, and product substitution is possible; the extent to which there are no-cost or low-cost opportunities for energy efficiency gains; the likely rate of technological change and its responsiveness to price signals; and the potential for emissions trading.

3. Equity.

Who should bear how much of the burden of emissions reduction — the industrialized countries who have been and are most responsible for emissions, or the developing countries that will be most responsible? Within the U.S., who should bear the burden? There is also a question of generational equity — how much the current generation should pay to avoid harm to future generations, particularly in countries where the current generation is poor, but also in wealthy countries, where future generations will presumably be even wealthier.

4. Technology.

New technologies will play a large role in reducing carbon emissions, but how will it happen, and how quickly? Is a continued or expanded government role in research appropriate? Will venture capital adequately support the development and deployment of technologies that could move us toward sustainability? And are government carrots or sticks necessary to ensure that flow of capital?

5. Governance.

How do individual nations acting in concert solve a global problem, particularly when there are potentially great competitive benefits for countries that do not participate in the solution? Some of those least responsible for the problem face the most severe consequences, while the countries that have been most responsible so far and that have the greatest financial ability to contribute to a solution are best able to adapt to severe climate change. The various solutions proposed will involve major transfers of resources among countries and may have major international trade implications. Enforcement of any international agreement will raise issues of loss of sovereignty. What institutional arrangements would allow the world to deal with these problems, and how and when can they be put in place?

Most remarkable about the 1998 Energy Policy Forum was the extent to which participants came to agree on the problems associated with the Kyoto Protocol and the actions that should be taken to deal with the problem of global climate change in general. The disparate views and vigorous exchanges that typically characterize the Energy Policy Forum were present, and there was clear disagreement on the wisdom of Kyoto, but in some areas the discussion converged toward a series of conclusions set out on the following pages.

Conclusions

1. Take a long term focus.

Climate change is a long term problem, and the focus should be on achieving sustainable levels of greenhouse gas concentrations at the least cost, not only on near-term emission reductions. Nevertheless, certain early actions, based on industry and other public suggestions, are desirable to develop institutions, mechanisms, technologies, and domestic and international support for long-term programs.

2. Do not reject the Kyoto Protocol nor submit it for ratification now.

Submission to the Senate and pre-emptive rejection of the Protocol would remove the U.S. from a political leadership role and put America at a competitive disadvantage in the continuing development of a sustainable energy system.

3. De-politicize the issue and educate the public.

U.S. political and intellectual leadership should undertake a high priority effort to increase public understanding of the issues, moderate the political aspects of the debate, and develop public consensus. One option for the Administration to consider is the establishment, in consultation with Congress, of a bi-partisan, very high level, Blue Ribbon Commission to lead in the development of a national consensus.

4. Establish bilateral programs with developing countries.

The Administration should work aggressively and quickly to establish bilateral carbon reduction programs with key developing countries such as China, India, and Brazil, stressing an early start toward a cost-effective long-term reduction in the dependence on fossil fuels.

After Kyoto: Are There Rational Pathways
to a Sustainable Global Energy System?

13

5. Increase R & D.

To reduce the cost of eventual stabilization of greenhouse gas concentrations, public and private spending for research and development of lower carbon and carbon-free fuels, technologies, and systems, including sequestration and end-use efficiency, should be increased significantly now. Coordination between public and private efforts should be enhanced. Commercial deployment should be left to market choices.

6. Set the rules for crediting early voluntary reductions.

The government, with broad industry and other public involvement, should quickly establish rules for crediting voluntary emissions reductions against any future standards.

7. Review barriers to innovation.

Many lower carbon technologies and more efficient systems are available, but long-standing laws and regulations often discourage their adoption. These barriers should be reviewed and, where more valuable objectives are not being served, should be removed promptly.

8. Ensure that policies are flexible.

Any governance mechanisms and policies should be sufficiently flexible to adapt to changing scientific knowledge and experience with implementation.

Session I: International Perspectives on the Kyoto Agreement

In December 1997, a new and controversial protocol to the Framework Convention on Climate Change signed in Rio in 1992, was negotiated during an international conference in Kyoto, Japan. Among its most contested provisions, particularly among some of its U.S. critics, is the Protocol's call for binding, developed country greenhouse gas emissions reductions on the order of 6-8% from 1990 levels between 2008 and 2012, while exempting developing countries from such commitments for the time being. In addition, the Protocol contains general provisions for the establishment of a global greenhouse gas emissions trading system and a "clean development mechanism" designed to facilitate cooperation and technical assistance between developed and developing countries. The design details of these new institutional structures are the subject of some controversy. The Forum heard various views on these issues from speakers representing several governments and from participants representing different perspectives and interests, both domestic and foreign.

Pathways to a Sustainable Energy Future

Are there rational pathways to a sustainable energy future? Does Kyoto represent an initial step in the right direction, or a wrong turn? These questions underlay discussions of the Kyoto Protocol, although cost, equity, and political considerations were often at the forefront.

In assessing Kyoto, a series of paradoxes appear to be inherent in the agreement. For example, the Protocol has been criticized on the one hand for going too far in the near-term demands it makes on industrialized countries, while it is at the same time criticized for doing little to address the long-term problem of stabilizing the concentration of greenhouse gases in the atmosphere. Also, the structure of the Kyoto Protocol took on a uniquely American style, whereby market-based solutions, such as emissions trading among industrialized countries, would take precedence over jointly agreed common measures to reduce emissions, as had been proposed by the European Union delegation. Yet, the Protocol finds itself in a more tenuous political situation in the U.S. than anywhere else in the world.

Paradoxes such as these, which currently characterize the climate debate, highlight key differences between climate change and other environmental issues—differences that make climate change inherently more challenging to address. Unlike U.S. legislation like the Clean Air Act or Superfund, the benefits of international climate legislation would be likely to accrue principally to citizens of future generations and in developing countries. Efforts to mitigate climate change, by seeking to reduce carbon emissions, also cut against the grain of the modern era, during which increasingly intense efforts have been made to exploit fossil fuels. Even the most rational pathway to a sustainable energy future, be that via the Kyoto Protocol or some other regime, must somehow surmount the political hindrances and momentum of the current system.

International Perspectives

Views on the Kyoto Protocol are as diverse as the nations that participated in the Kyoto Conference. International perspectives on the Protocol reflect the participating nations' cultures and stages of development, and the outcomes that they anticipate as a result of the agreement's implementation. This section considers a variety of international perspectives on the Protocol, as characterized by Forum participants.

From the perspective of some Japanese observers, the Kyoto accord represents a historic development in that it was an initial, concrete step toward the control of global greenhouse gas emissions. As such, of course, it is neither perfect nor adequate nor equitable. Its greatest value lies in its initiation of concrete actions.

In many respects, the implications of the Kyoto Protocol for Japan are more severe than they are for other developed countries. Since Japan and Japanese industry are already relatively efficient, achieving a net emissions reduction of 30% from business-as-usual projections over the coming decade, as Japan's commitment demands, will be difficult and expensive. Nonetheless, the Japanese government believes that implementation must proceed since the Protocol is now the only feasible means of stabilizing the atmosphere. Thus, in its view, it is of the highest importance that the major industrialized nations accept and ratify the Protocol.

The Japanese government is instituting several measures aimed at meeting its Kyoto commitments. First, it is setting progressive standards for industrial energy efficiency. For example, the government is now seeking to identify the most efficient auto producer in the country. The energy efficiency level of that producer will be raised by some measure and set as the standard that the industry as a whole will be required to attain over the coming decade. Furthermore, Japanese industry as a whole is being encouraged to make a voluntary commitment of 1% annual reduction in energy use for the foreseeable future. The government is also encouraging lifestyle and behavioral changes to improve energy efficiency. For example, thermostats in all government buildings will be set at 28 degrees Celsius. The government is considering new energy efficiency regulations and restrictions on consumer products and is working to better inform the public at large on the issues of climate change and energy efficiency.

Yet, having said this, the Japanese government would find itself in an exceptionally difficult position should the U.S. not ratify the Protocol. Whether Japan would be able to ratify the agreement itself in that case remains an open question.

Major developing countries have entirely different views on the Protocol. Consider, for example, the case of China, the world's largest developing country whose average annual growth has exceeded 9% on average for the past 20 years. Despite the country's tremendous recent growth, 60 million Chinese remain in poverty. It was suggested that, in order to fully appreciate conditions in China, one must look beyond the rapid economic growth and improving living standards occurring in

many of China's major cities. Many rural dwellers have yet to share in
China's recent and dramatic progress.

China's growth and industrialization have, of course, brought urgent
environmental challenges, some of which are directly related to the
rapid growth in the country's energy use, particularly in the nation's
low-efficiency coal-fired electricity. Nearly half of China's land mass
feels the impacts of coal use through serious local air pollution and acid
deposition. While the government is making a concerted effort to
address energy-related environmental problems, for instance through
investments in renewable energy and efficiency projects, expected
annual energy growth of 3-4% over the next fifteen years is expected to
be fueled primarily by coal.

One of the most promising signs with respect to China's energy-eco-
nomic situation is the fact that incomes are now growing more rapidly
than energy use. Nonetheless, on average, one kilogram of energy
inputs produces 70 cents of economic output in China, while in U.S.
the same amount of energy produces an average of $3.20. There are
clearly opportunities for improvement of China's energy productivity.
On a per capita basis, however, the average American consumes nearly
12 times as much energy as the average Chinese.

The Chinese head of delegation at Kyoto declared that China would
take steps to reduce carbon emissions voluntarily, despite its resistance
to making formal commitments, basing its opposition on two grounds.
First, from an economic perspective, China simply cannot afford to take
actions that might dampen its continued growth. Second, on
moral/ethical grounds, China simply refuses to endorse greenhouse
gas reduction obligations for developing countries in the absence of
real commitments and assistance from the developed nations. Why,
they ask, should major developing countries such as China and India
consent to penalizing their economic growth when their per capita
emissions are so much lower than those of the countries that actually
created the problem in the first place?

Some Europeans echo developing countries' views in their own perspectives on the Kyoto Protocol. An important fact, in their opinion, is
often lost in the debates concerning developed countries' greenhouse
gas reduction commitments under the Protocol. That is, through the
ratification of the Rio Convention, over 100 national governments—

AFTER KYOTO: ARE THERE RATIONAL PATHWAYS
TO A SUSTAINABLE GLOBAL ENERGY SYSTEM?

19

including that of the U.S.—have ratified the precautionary principle. In brief, this provision states that nations "should take precautionary measures to anticipate, prevent, or minimize" climate change and its adverse effects, and that "lack of full scientific certainty should not be a reason for postponing such measures." Under the Framework Convention, industrialized countries agreed they must take the lead with regard to actions to mitigate climate change; the fact that these countries have thus far not lived up to this commitment deprives them of the right to insist on developing country commitments at this stage.

Moreover, industrialized countries are poised to fail to meet their commitments under the Framework Convention to reduce their greenhouse gas emissions to 1990 levels by the year 2000. While the member states of the European Union will aim for an 8% emissions reduction from 1990 levels in the target period of 2008-2012, some argue that this target will prove unrealistic. Overall, the EU is now 5% above its 1990 levels, and the "low hanging fruit"—the inefficient power plants and industrial facilities in eastern Germany that provided relatively inexpensive opportunities for carbon emissions reductions—has already been seized. Furthermore, Europeans' willingness to brake future economic growth in the interest of the global climate seems unlikely, given the sluggish growth that Europe has experienced in the 1990s.

By this assessment, the Kyoto Protocol cannot achieve its targets. Even assuming ratification, implementation of the Protocol could not proceed until the various questions regarding specific articles of the agreement were addressed satisfactorily. Subject of the most intense debate are the Protocol's provisions regarding the three "flexible mechanisms": joint implementation, the clean development mechanism, and emissions trading. Addressing these concerns would effectively forestall action for an indefinite period, making the likelihood that the protocol would achieve its goals in the desired time frame even more remote. While there is already voluntary action occurring in the private sector, this action alone will fall far short in the absence of intergovernmental action.

Intergovernmental action may be effectively forestalled by opposition to the Kyoto agreement in the U.S. Congress. While ratification of the agreement by the U.S. Senate may be in question, the Administration, having signed the Kyoto Protocol, is on record in favor of a binding international climate agreement. In its efforts to build support for its position among Congressional and industry leaders, the U.S. Administration is focusing on a number of major issues, such as design features of a proposed international emissions trading regime that could greatly reduce the costs of treaty compliance. Some models suggest, for instance, that savings of up to 85% of the costs associated with the desired reductions could be achieved through a trading regime alone—assuming a well-designed system.

Also, the Administration is working to secure the participation of major developing countries in the Kyoto Protocol; the failure to engage these countries to date in a meaningful way has been a major source of Congressional opposition to the Protocol. While developing countries clearly should not shoulder as great a burden as developed countries, from the standpoint of the Administration, there ought nonetheless to be a basic commitment to a deflection in some measure from base case scenario trajectories. Forum participants felt that the U.S. should work to engage major developing countries bilaterally in arrangements outside of the Kyoto Protocol designed to reduce greenhouse gas emissions. These relationships could establish a foundation of trust and cooperation that might then form the basis of future developing country participation in the formal Kyoto framework. Moreover, successful bilateral actions of this nature might help to allay Congressional fears concerning U.S. participation in formalized institutional structures such as the Kyoto Protocol that aim to address climate change multilaterally.

Recognizing that the ratification of the Kyoto Protocol is unlikely in the near future, the Administration has proposed a series of domestic measures aimed to reduce U.S. emissions and improve energy efficiency. This includes a proposed $6.3 billion package of tax credits and incentives for firms that take early action to reduce their greenhouse gas emissions, even in the absence of treaty commitments. Furthermore, the President recently sent legislation to Congress addressing electricity restructuring; some believe that, if passed, this bill could make a major contribution to energy efficiency through the broadening of competition in U.S. energy markets.

In the Administration's estimation, public attitudes in the U.S. reflect a growing public concern over climate change, which may be related to

AFTER KYOTO: ARE THERE RATIONAL PATHWAYS
TO A SUSTAINABLE GLOBAL ENERGY SYSTEM?

21

this year's strong El Niño and the fact that each month of 1998 has been the hottest on record. This growth in awareness, which might be taken as a promising sign, also provides cause for concern. That is, to the extent that the current level of awareness is linked to this year's El Niño and to extreme weather events, a single cold winter or mild year may easily dampen public consciousness. There is, perhaps now more than ever, a need for more concerted efforts at public information and education regarding the state of knowledge of climate change.

Session II: Governance
and Policy Instruments

The task of defining a governance path and policy instruments that might lead the world to a sustainable energy future—a task that has been daunting enough in the past—has grown significantly more difficult today. Throughout the world, a new political and economic order is evolving. Markets are being deregulated, privatized, liberalized, and globalized as countries of both the developed and developing world rely to a greater extent on markets rather than government to meet societal needs. At the same time, central governments have devolved decision-making to lower levels of authority. And, by becoming more democratic, governments have taken on a greater responsibility to justify and gain public support before taking policy steps—particularly those that might add costs to essential energy infrastructures. Governments now exercise far less control over domestic and international economic activities than they did even a decade ago.

Cooperation is necessary to an unprecedented degree, since so many problems are now beyond individual nations' control. And yet, cooperation is more difficult than before; in the post-Cold War period, economic rivalry has in many cases become more important than strategic alliances between states. For that matter, several new forces for conflict and for cooperation have been set in motion in the international system and continue to unfold. For example, regional differences and trade rivalries could become more deeply engrained, driving nations apart rather than toward a sense of common purpose. On the other hand, accelerating advances in information and telecommunications technologies might facilitate the development of shared, global values and understanding. These and other major trends could have significant bearing on the prospects for international cooperation to stabilize the global climate.

Global Climate Policy: The Art of the Long View

Whether one approves of the product of the Kyoto Conference or not, the Protocol does follow the basic pattern established through all of the major climate negotiations to date. That is, its focus is on short-term targets and timetables; binding limits for industrialized countries only; voluntary/joint implementation programs for others; recognition of the great potential of "market mechanisms"; and a lack of focus on the details of treaty enforcement.

In the light of these aspects of the Kyoto Protocol, there are several actions that must be taken at the upcoming 1998 conference in Buenos Aires to improve the long-term prospects for the effectiveness of the agreement and for climate protection. First of all, the most important developing countries, such as China, India, Mexico, and Brazil, must be brought on board, since this small set of countries will soon account for over 50% of global greenhouse gas emissions. Moreover, these countries present many opportunities for low-cost emissions reductions. This fact relates to a more serious problem associated with the failure to bring developing countries into the Kyoto Protocol—namely, that of "carbon leakage." That is, if developed countries are required to reduce their emissions while developing countries' emissions remain unrestricted, there is a likelihood that some carbon-intensive industries will relocate their operations to developing countries.

Also, participating nations must establish rules and institutions to address non-compliance and workable rules for emissions trading, which could yield enormous cost savings in the implementation of the Protocol. Recent estimates suggest that emissions trading among industrialized countries alone could lead to significant cost savings over implementation without emissions trading—estimated by some models at 2% of global GDP annually.

Finally, and most importantly, nations need to articulate and focus on long-term goals, rather than the short-term objectives that have been the subject of the negotiations thus far. As a long-term problem, climate change requires that policy-makers take a long view in responding to the challenge, which would include a sustained commitment to scientific research and public education. Many economists now argue that the most viable path to long-term stabilization of the atmosphere allows greenhouse gas emissions to continue rising in the short-term, while new institutions are built, technologies developed, and capital investments made. Industry especially requires both a long lead time and a strong sense of governments' long-term commitment to the problem in order to begin the necessary capital stock turnover that will ultimately reduce global greenhouse gas emissions.

Assessing Alternative Policy Approaches
to Carbon Emissions Reduction

While some Forum participants stressed the shortcomings inherent in the Kyoto Protocol, others argued that, flawed as it may be, the agreement does comprise the fundamental policy infrastructure needed for effective action. According to those who expressed optimism concerning its potential effectiveness, the Protocol establishes a flexible framework within which any of a series of policy models might be employed.

A combination of four standard policy instruments can be accommodated in the Kyoto framework. Command and control measures, such as codes, standards, and regulations regarding energy use, are frequently favored by the European Union and Japan; carbon taxes might also be effectively employed to curtail atmospheric concentrations of carbon and favor lower carbon fossil fuels; international emissions trading, favored by the U.S., could potentially lower the costs of atmospheric stabilization significantly; finally, voluntary measures, the most appealing instrument to key industries (particularly electric utilities), hold great potential and have yet to be fully explored. Several participants stressed that industry would continue to take actions that reduced greenhouse gas emissions aggressively, provided an incentive structure were in place giving industry credit for early action. This is not currently the case in the U.S., where the absence of such incentives may be a factor in the continued rise in carbon emissions.

In any case, policies and incentives adopted in response to climate change, whether in the framework of the Kyoto Protocol or otherwise, should strive to satisfy a set of fundamental criteria. In the opinion of several Forum participants, governments should observe a "Hippocratic principle" in attempting to respond to climate change; that is, government should avoid intervening in ways that are likely to cause harm by imposing high costs or regulations that may ultimately impede progress on the issue. Preferably, in the process of removing barriers, government should adopt a technologically neutral stance that will allow the market to choose the most effective means of achieving emissions reduction goals. Thus, a major role of government should be the establishment of clear and enforceable "rules of the road" and administrative procedures that will facilitate efficiency in the market. Also, government should strive for broad coverage, addressing a wide range of sources and emitters including historical high-emitters as well as rapidly growing firms and industries. Finally, any regime that is adopted should be true to the spirit of the Protocol, meaning that it seeks real emissions reductions and is flexible in implementation.

Crafting the U.S. Response to Kyoto

Questions of policy design aside, what level of response to climate change is appropriate now? How should a responsible government act, given that its efforts to curtail greenhouse gas emissions are likely to have high short-run costs and yield benefits that are uncertain and distant, both temporally and geographically. Climate and energy models designed to aid policy development often seem to serve interest group politics by providing results that can be "dialed-on-demand" in the view of some observers. The U.S. Congress has taken a large measure of criticism for its unwillingness to act, but it is fair to say that members of Congress are responsive to the opinions of their constituents. Thus, Congress' attitude really reflects the general reluctance of the American people to tax their own lifestyles or, in the view of some, to compromise U.S. sovereignty, especially when the benefits and beneficiaries are neither clear nor present. To a large extent, Congressional opposition even to energy R&D stems from the perceived linkage between research spending and the climate change issue.

Some members of Congress who attended the Kyoto Conference claimed to be shocked by what they witnessed. As far as they were concerned, the meeting and the Protocol were, at root, mechanisms to transfer income to developing countries hidden under a veneer of concern for the global climate. By their reckoning, and by that of many other Americans, it would be the height of irresponsibility for the U.S. government to ratify the Kyoto Protocol, considering its vagueness, inherent limitations, and hidden agendas. Based on this assessment, some Forum participants suggested that the Kyoto Protocol be submitted to the Senate for ratification without delay, so that the treaty could be defeated, effectively wiping the slate clean and clearing the way for an entirely different international approach to the problem. A large majority of Forum participants, however, warned of the dangers inherent in this approach. Should it defeat the treaty, the U.S. Senate would not only be killing the Kyoto Protocol but also uprooting an important international, political learning process and thereby seriously compromising the future of U.S. leadership and prestige.

Also, it is important to realize that climate change, like all big, new issues, will take time to jell and capture the attention of both elites and the public. Some participants argued that, before entering into a binding treaty commitment that may well prove ineffective in the long run, it would be wiser for governments first to adopt lower-risk, lower-cost measures that may be highly effective. For instance the potential for markets, incentives, and voluntary measures to spur innovation and emissions reduction has not been explored very deeply thus far. Some felt that measures such as these represent a more appropriate way to get off the mark in addressing the problem at present; in the long term, they may even prove themselves capable of surpassing international treaties and organizations in their ability to deal with climate change.

Taking these factors into consideration, several Forum participants suggested that delaying the Kyoto Protocol's submission to the Senate might be the wisest course of action for the time being. Delaying submission until after the 2000 election may help to elicit a better-informed and less politically-charged Senate vote than is likely to occur now.

Session III: Economics

The role of economic models and analysis is central to the debate surrounding the Kyoto Protocol, attempting to bring rigor and internal consistency to the discussion. There is, however, still a substantial amount of work to be done in this regard. Relatively little is known, for example, about the redistribution of costs, benefits, and income that the implementation of the Kyoto Protocol might entail. Nonetheless, as economists work to improve their quantification of costs and benefits, their efforts further a thinking and learning process that contributes, in itself, to progress in addressing climate change.

The Economics of Climate Action: Minimizing Costs by Maximizing Flexibility

Economic models and analyses suggest that there are two elements essential to cost-effective emissions reduction. First, actions must be flexible and market-based, to ensure the most efficient means of reduction; second, actions must be global in order to be effective. The climate change problem is characterized by the fact that greenhouse gas emissions have the same effect regardless of how, where, and, to a large extent, when they occur. This suggests that, in designing responses to the problem, flexibility be incorporated in each of these three dimensions.

For example, the choice of a multi-year emissions budget period with allowances for the banking of emissions reductions, constitute key elements of "when" flexibility. Such provisions could help to mitigate costs by

permitting reductions at times when they are less costly. The inclusion in
the Protocol of carbon sinks and of a set of six primary greenhouse gases,
weighted in relation to their importance to the problem, are key aspects of
"what" flexibility. In this regard, a major aim of the U.S. was to have the
Protocol stipulate that nations would reduce their overall emissions to
specified levels, but without requiring specific reductions for specific gases.

Finally, the inclusion of structures such as the "clean development
mechanism" and international trading of greenhouse gases are critical
forms of "where" flexibility that will help to facilitate the lowest cost emissions reduction pathway. It is important to note, however, that institutions such as international emissions trading regimes have proven controversial among countries of both the developed and the developing
world. Critics of emissions trading view trading schemes as the industrialized world's effort to "export" its commitment to address the problem.
Equity-based critiques such as these underscore the fact that economic
efficiency alone may be insufficient as a rationale for the establishment
of new international institutions to address climate change.

Economic models and analysis also indicate that, as a global problem,
climate change requires a global solution. Model results show that,
around the year 2015, the majority of the world's carbon emissions will
come from developing countries, assuming a business-as-usual scenario.
Thus, without the participation of the developing world, there can be no
effective climate protection. Moreover, developing country participation
would permit relatively low-cost emissions reductions to be recognized as
a substitute for more expensive reductions in industrialized countries.

In short, if efforts to mitigate climate change are both flexible in
implementation and global in scope, economic analysis shows that the
net costs of greenhouse gas emissions reductions could potentially be
small. According to at least one model, emissions trading among industrialized countries alone would reduce costs by approximately 50%;
with full world participation in emissions trading, costs could be
reduced by still another 50% to about $12 billion worldwide in 2010.
Likely future developments such as the deregulation of the electric utility industry in the U.S. and other countries, and more efficient use of
carbon sinks, would be likely to reduce costs of compliance even further. On the other hand, if designed and implemented improperly, flexibility mechanisms might result in even higher than expected costs.

AFTER KYOTO: ARE THERE RATIONAL PATHWAYS
TO A SUSTAINABLE GLOBAL ENERGY SYSTEM?

31

Several energy models also yield strikingly similar insights regarding the optimal, least-cost pathway to long-term stabilization of the atmosphere. A global strategy that permits emissions to rise in the short-term (e.g., over the period from the present to 2015), during which global incomes rise and significant new energy technology investments would be made, might yield desired atmospheric carbon concentrations more effectively and at far lower total cost than strategies focusing on short-term greenhouse gas reductions. While some believe this approach countenances delay with no guarantee of future action, the failure of the Kyoto Protocol to accommodate this insight underlies many economists' and business leaders' opposition to it.

A related point is made by some to allay concerns about the projected growth of carbon emissions in developing countries and about these countries not accepting near-term emissions reduction targets. As Figure 1 indicates, in the early stages of economic growth, energy consumption normally grows more rapidly than national income. But as growth continues, energy efficiency increases and energy intensive industries become less prominent. According to this argument, a natural reduction in carbon emissions per capita will accompany economic growth.

Figure 1: Energy Intensity

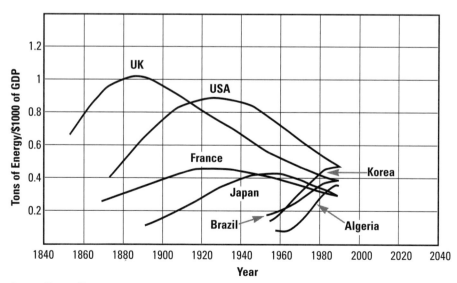

Source: Energy 21

AFTER KYOTO: ARE THERE RATIONAL PATHWAYS
TO A SUSTAINABLE GLOBAL ENERGY SYSTEM?

33

Session IV: Technology

Technology is a central issue in all discussions of climate change, as are the related issues of governance and market failures that may hinder innovation and deployment of new technologies. What actions might be taken to exploit more fully technology's potential in addressing the problem? Certainly an examination of recent successes and failures is merited. Government efforts over the past three decades have produced mixed results. Programs aimed at promoting the development and use of renewable and nuclear energy have met with some success, albeit at a high cost, while the effort to commercialize synthetic fuels was a failure. Programs to develop and commercialize clean coal technologies were moderately successful but largely overwhelmed by fuel switching when market based clean air regulations were adopted. At the same time, private investments in natural gas systems, spurred in large part by technological advances, removal of some government restrictions, and the tightening of clean air standards, have grown significantly in recent years. This experience shows that the roles of government and markets in stimulating technological change can be effective when they are complementary but can be counterproductive when government actions go beyond research and the removal of barriers and seek to commercialize specific technologies.

Forum participants differed in their views on the respective roles of governments and markets in spurring technological change. Most agreed, however, that the timetable specified in the Kyoto Protocol was too short to permit the investments and regulatory changes necessary for the widespread deployment of new, low-carbon energy technologies.

Removing Regulatory Barriers to Technological Change

Even though the current regulatory structure is now undergoing major change, several of the regime's long-standing rules still may impede the deployment of new energy technologies such as those mentioned above. For example, the monopoly protection previously afforded to electricity generators in exchange for reliable service made it difficult for new service providers to gain access to the system. The challenge to policy makers is to remove unnecessary regulatory strictures and to craft modern approaches that will allow the market to spur higher levels of efficiency by taking advantage of new technologies that are now commercially available.

For example, as Figure 2 shows, where existing conventional thermal electric plants convert fuel at an average 33% efficiency and emit the remaining energy to the environment as waste heat and pollution, all new plants exceed this efficiency rate. New combined heat and power plants have a conversion efficiency that exceeds 90%. The carbon dioxide reduction associated with substituting combined heat and power for a conventional plant is 50%, assuming no fuel switch is involved. If, as is typically the case, the new plants are gas fired, the reduction can be as great as 80%. The reductions in many key air pollutants can be even more substantial.

Figure 2: Generating Efficiencies of Various Technologies Today

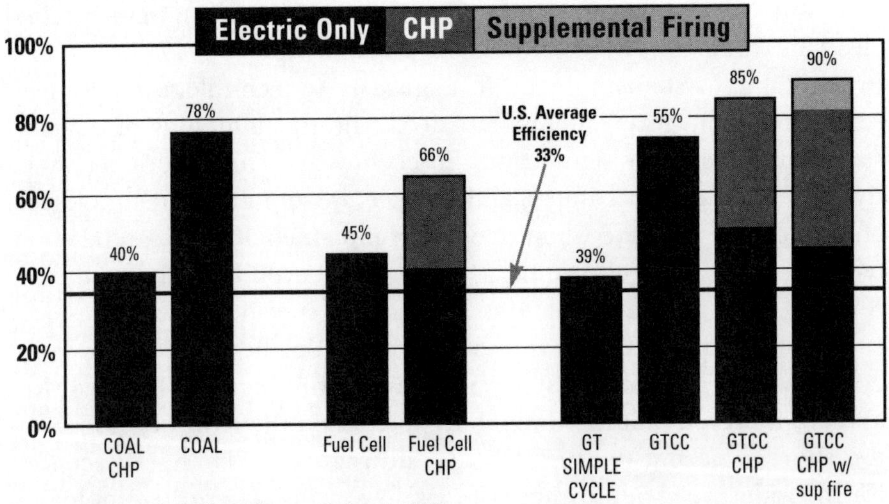

Source: *Turning Off the Heat*, Thomas R. Casten, 1998.

AFTER KYOTO: ARE THERE RATIONAL PATHWAYS
TO A SUSTAINABLE GLOBAL ENERGY SYSTEM?

35

Environmental regulations, such as input-based rather than performance-based standards, and the grandfathering of old plants also provide disincentives for investments in new, more efficient energy technologies. Today, for instance, 26 years after the passage of the Clean Air Act, two-thirds of all U.S. generating capacity was built prior to the Act and could be economically replaced in the absence of environmental regulatory barriers. Performance based standards for air pollutants that applied to power plants would fix the problem, by prompting energy companies to seize cost-savings opportunities that greatly reduced their emissions.

Many Forum participants felt that the Administration's proposed legislation restructuring the electricity industry was a positive step in this direction, and one that would ultimately result in more efficient energy use and lower carbon emissions. Yet they cautioned that the short-term effects of deregulation and restructuring could be higher emissions, as the industry's current low-cost producers, Midwest coal utilities whose capital is now fully-amortized, would be able to extend their reach beyond their current service areas. Others contended, however, that transmission constraints would prevent this outcome.

Some participants argued that a departure from the conventional thinking about the relationship between energy and climate is also necessary to catalyze a regulatory and technological transition. The predominant view holds that climate protection requires a dramatic change in energy production and use, which in turn is likely to entail higher energy costs, losses of jobs, and sluggish economic growth. Under this assumption, it would indeed make sense to delay climate action until there is much greater certainty regarding the causes and extent of the problem, and then to act only in concert with others, since being the first to act would likely result in self-imposed economic penalties.

An alternative perspective suggests that saving energy saves money and that saving energy could occur quickly and profitably if regulatory barriers to such actions were removed. These actions would boost the economy, while addressing the climate change problem incidentally. Moreover, being the first to initiate energy saving measures would confer an economic advantage rather than a handicap. Under this scenario, scientific certainties and uncertainties associated with climate change would be irrelevant.

There are many feasible intervention points in the current energy system that could be used to seize some of the opportunities available. Technology offers means of intervening to save energy profitably in at least three key ways: by reducing carbon intensity through the broader use of natural gas and renewable energy; by improving energy conversion efficiency, for instance through the use of combined heat and power; and by improving energy end-use efficiency. Design for whole system optimization, in effect integrating design considerations in each of the three areas discussed above, could produce even more substantial gains of efficiency and profitability.

While numerous opportunities exist in each of these areas, several types of market failure currently prevent major savings from being purchased in each of these areas. Capital misallocation, for instance, often occurs because most energy equipment purchases are based on first cost alone. For example, thicker electrical wiring in commercial buildings is usually not installed due to its higher up-front cost. Similarly, regulatory failures prevent changes that could yield profitable energy savings. For example, almost every utility in the world is rewarded for selling more energy and penalized for cutting customers' bills. Also, perverse incentives reward architects and engineers according to what they spend, rather than what they save. False price signals, distorted by subsidies and unpriced externalities, skew the system further, imposing additional barriers to positive changes. In short, according to this view, regulatory and market failures constitute some of the most significant obstacles to the technological transformation of the energy system.

Stimulating Energy Research and Development

Minimizing the costs of stabilizing atmospheric concentrations of greenhouse gases will require a long-term strategy focusing public and private R&D investments on the development and deployment of low-carbon and carbon-free energy technologies during the next century. Yet, even though many economists and policy-makers agree on this point, the fact is that both public and private sector R&D investments are declining in most industrialized countries.

What drivers underlie this disconnect between policy objectives and R&D investments? In 1996, the President's Committee of Advisors on

AFTER KYOTO: ARE THERE RATIONAL PATHWAYS
TO A SUSTAINABLE GLOBAL ENERGY SYSTEM?

37

Science and Technology (PCAST) sought to explain this phenomenon and offered recommendations in response to it.

The PCAST panel found several noteworthy trends in U.S. energy R&D investment. For example, total U.S. private sector energy R&D fell in real terms from $4.4 billion in 1985 to $2.6 billion in 1994. R&D funding by the 112 largest electric utilities fell by 38% between 1993 and 1996 alone, while R&D investments of the four largest U.S. oil firms fell by over 50%. Hardest hit of all has been broad-based, long-term research. Chief among the causes for these declines is the deregulation and restructuring of the energy industries, which has led to increased price competition and an aversion to long-term, higher-risk R&D investments. A related cause is the growing pressure on energy companies from financial markets and stockholders for higher short-run returns, which increases companies' reluctance to invest in R&D projects from which the payoffs are far in the future and/or uncertain.

Figure 3: Research and Development Investments

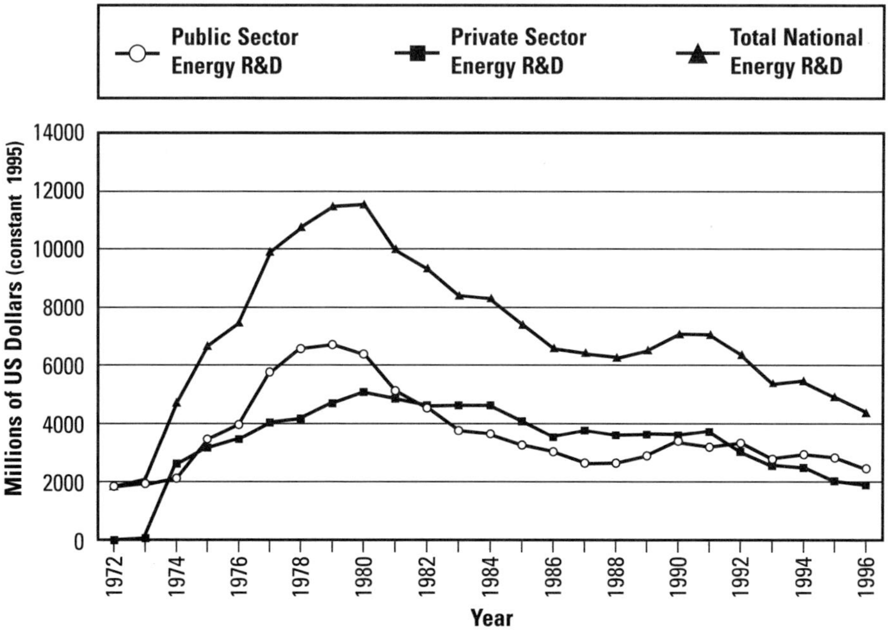

Source: "Federal Energy Research and Development for the Challenges of the Twenty-First Century," Presidents's Council of Advisors on Science and Technology, 1997.

The study concluded that current federal energy R&D are not commensurate in scale or scope with the energy challenges and opportunities that the 21st century will present, especially considering the investments that the private sector will be likely to make. The inadequacy of federal R&D investment is especially acute in relation to the challenge of responding to global climate change. Since climate change is a long-term, societal problem demanding major up-front investments with a distant payoff, government is better suited than the market to respond.

As history has shown, the economic benefits of new energy technology investments are potentially great. The broader deployment of new technologies could reduce the costs associated with energy supply and end use, increase U.S. high-technology exports, and reduce the nation's high dependence on oil imports. From an environmental standpoint, new energy technologies could also reduce the concentration of greenhouse gases in the atmosphere and improve local air quality, enhancing the prospects for environmentally-sustainable economic development.

Yet, while market mechanisms may contribute significantly to improvements in energy efficiency and climate change mitigation, the market alone will not be able to address the energy-related technological challenges that the U.S. and the world will face in coming decades. While technology commercialization is best left to the private sector, the role of government on the "front end," as a sponsor of basic and applied energy R&D, is growing more rather than less important. Current levels of federal energy R&D investments are inadequate, given the magnitude of the task at hand.

AFTER KYOTO: ARE THERE RATIONAL PATHWAYS
TO A SUSTAINABLE GLOBAL ENERGY SYSTEM?

39

Forum Participants

P. J. Adam
Chairman and Chief Executive
Officer
Black & Veatch
8400 Ward Parkway
P.O. Box 8405
Kansas City, MO 64114

Alvin L. Alm
Executive Vice President
The Columbus Group
2111 Wilson Boulevard
Suite 1200
Arlington, VA 22201

Merribel S. Ayres
President
Lighthouse Energy Group
2501 M Street, NW
Suite 500
Washington, DC 20037

Richard E. Ayres
Partner
Howrey & Simon
1299 Pennsylvania Avenue, NW
Washington, DC 20004-2402

The Honorable Vicky A. Bailey
Commissioner
Federal Energy Regulatory
Commission
888 First Street, NE
Suite 11B
Washington, DC 20426

Michael L. Beatty
Federal Representative
Western Interstate Energy
Board
10 Boulder Crescent
Suite 303
Colorado Springs, CO 80903

Roger A. Berliner
Managing Partner
Brady & Berliner
1225 19th Street, NW
Suite 800
Washington, DC 20036

Ellen Berman
President
Consumer Energy Council of
  America Research Foundation
2000 L Street, NW
Suite 802
Washington, DC 20036

Peter D. Blair
Executive Director
Sigma Xi, The Scientific
  Research Society
P.O. Box 13975
99 Alexander Drive
Research Triangle Park, NC 27709

Peter Bradford
Energy Advisor
Fellow, Regulatory Assistance
  Project
P.O. Box 497
Bradford Road
Route 11
Peru, VT 05152-0497

John E. Bryson
Chairman of the Board and CEO
Edison International
2244 Walnut Grove Avenue
P.O. Box 800
Rosemead, CA 91770

Van Bussmann
Corporate Economist
Chrysler Corporation
1000 Chrysler Drive
Auburn Hills, MI 48326-2766

Thomas Casten
President & CEO
Trigen Energy Corporation
One Water Street
White Plains, NY 10601

Red Cavaney
President and CEO
American Petroleum Institute
1220 L Street, NW
Washington, DC 20005

John F. Clarke
Manager
Public Sector Energy Accounts
Battelle Pacific Northwest
  National Laboratory
370 L'Enfant Promenade
901 D Street, SW
Suite 900
Washington, DC 20024

Greg Conlon
Commissioner
California Public Utilities
  Commission
State Building
505 Van Ness Avenue
San Francisco, CA 94102

AFTER KYOTO: ARE THERE RATIONAL PATHWAYS
TO A SUSTAINABLE GLOBAL ENERGY SYSTEM?

41

Benjamin S. Cooper
Executive Director
Association of Oil Pipelines
1101 Vermont Avenue, NW
Suite 604
Washington, DC 20005

Chester L. Cooper
Deputy Director
Emerging Technologies
Battelle Pacific Northwest
    National Laboratory
901 D Street, SW
Suite 900
Washington, DC 20024

Loren C. Cox
Associate Director
MIT Center for Energy &
    Environmental Policy
    Research
350 Belaire Court
Punta Gorda, FL 33950

Charles B. Curtis
Hogan & Hartson
555 13th Street, NW
Washington, DC 20004-1109

Etienne Deffarges
Head of Energy and Chemical
    Practice
Booz • Allen & Hamilton Inc.
101 California Street
Suite 3300
San Francisco, CA 94111

William E. Dickenson
President
Putnam, Hayes & Bartlett, Inc.
1776 Eye Street, NW
Washington, DC 20006

J.W. Dickey
Chief Operating Officer
Tennessee Valley Authority
400 West Summit Hill Drive
Knoxville, TN 37902

Paul Dragoumis
President
Paul Dragoumis Associates, Inc.
P.O. Box 5
Cabin John, MD 20818-0015

Theodore R. Eck
Senior Economic Consultant
Amoco
271 New Boston Road
Norwich, VT 05055

Patricia Eckert
Advisor, Office of the President
SRI Consulting
333 Ravenswood Avenue
Menlo Park, CA 94025

Juan Eibenschutz
Subdirector de Distribucion Y
    Comercializacion
Luz & Fuerza Del Centro
Melchor Ocampo 171-8
11379 Mexico, D.F.

Cheryl M. Foley
Vice President, General Counsel
& Corporate Secretary
Cinergy Corporation
221 East Fourth Street
Atrium 30
Cincinnati, OH 45202

Dirk Forrister
Chair
White House Climate Change
Task Force
734 Jackson Place NW
Washington, DC 20503

Dr. Jeffrey Frankel
Member
Council of Economic Advisors
17th & Pennsylvania Avenue, NW
Room 314
Washington, DC 20502

William Fulkerson
Senior Fellow
Joint Institute for Energy &
Environment
600 Henley Street
Suite 34
Knoxville, TN 37996-4138

David Garman
Chief of Staff
Office of Senator Frank H.
Murkowski
Energy and Natural Resources
Committee
U.S. Senate
Washington, DC 20510

John H. Gibbons
Former Science and Technology
Advisor to the President
P.O. Box 379
The Plains, VA 20198

Lorne Gordon
President and CEO
LORAM Corporation
P.O. Box 2550
Suite 3000
707 8th Avenue, SW
Calgary, Alberta
Canada T2P 2M7

Hal Harvey
Executive Director
Energy Foundation
Presidio Building 1012
Torney Avenue
San Francisco, CA 94129

Robert A. Hefner III
Chairman
The GHK Companies
6305 Waterford Boulevard
Suite 470
Oklahoma City, OK 73118

J. Stephen Henderson
Principal
Putnam, Hayes & Bartlett
1776 Eye Street, NW
Washington, DC 20006

Dale E. Heydlauff
Vice President-Environmental
   Affairs
American Electric Power
1 Riverside Plaza
19th Floor
Columbus, OH 43215

Yasushi Hieda
Manager
Tokyo Electric Power Company,
   Incorporated
1901 L Street, NW
Suite 720
Washington, DC 20036

William W. Hogan
Lucius N. Littauer Professor of
   Public Policy and Administration
Kennedy School of Government
Harvard University
79 John F. Kennedy Street
Cambridge, MA 02138

Dr. John Holdren
Teresa and John Heinz Professor
   of Environmental Policy
Kennedy School of Government
Harvard University
79 John F. Kennedy Street L3
Cambridge, MA 02138

Sheila S. Hollis
Partner-In-Charge, Washington
   Office
Duane, Morris & Heckscher, LLP
1667 K Street, NW
Suite 700
Washington, DC 20006-1608

Paul Holtberg
Group Manager
Baseline/Gas Resource
   Analytical Center
Gas Research Institute
1600 Wilson Boulevard
Suite 900
Arlington, VA 22209

Angelina Howard
Senior Vice President, Industry
   Communications
Nuclear Energy Institute
1776 Eye Street, NW
Suite 400
Washington, DC 20006

H.M. Hubbard
President and CEO (Retired)
PICHTR
3245 Newland Street
Wheat Ridge, CO 80033

Toshio Inoue
Chief Economist
Cosmo Oil Co., Ltd.
1-1-1, Shibaura, Minato-ku
Tokyo 105, Japan

Michael Jefferson
Deputy Secretary General
World Energy Council
34 Street James's Street
London, SW1A 1HD
United Kingdom

Guo Jing
Second Secretary
Embassy of Peoples Republic of
  China
2300 Connecticut Avenue, NW
Washington, DC 20008

Frederick E. John
Senior Vice President
Public Policy and Law
Pacific Enterprises
555 West 5th Street
ML29H2
Los Angeles, CA 90013

The Honorable J. Bennett Johnston
Johnston & Associates
1455 Pennsylvania Avenue, NW
Suite 200
Washington, DC 20004

The Honorable Takayuki Kimura
Ambassador Extraordinary and
  Plenipotentiary
International Trade and
  Economic Affairs
Global Environmental Affairs
Ministry of Foreign Affairs
2-1 Kasunigaseki
2 Chome Chiyodaku
Tokyo 100-0013, Japan

Wilfrid L. Kohl
Director, Energy &
  Environment Program
Johns Hopkins University SAIS
1619 Massachusetts Avenue, NW
Washington, DC 20036

Thomas R. Kuhn
President
Edison Electric Institute
701 Pennsylvania Avenue, NW
Washington, DC 20004-2696

Jonathan Lash
President
World Resources Institute
1709 New York Avenue, NW
Washington, DC 20006

Lester Lave
Professor of Economics
Carnegie Mellon University
Graduate School of Industrial
  Administration
Pittsburgh, PA 15213

Kenneth L. Lay
Chairman and CEO
Enron Corp.
1400 Smith Street
Houston, TX 77251-1188

Tanneguy Le Maréchal
Electricite de France
32 Rue Monceau
F-75008 Paris
Codex 08
France

P. Barrie Leay
Chairman
Energy Federation of New
  Zealand
P.O. Box 17072
Karori, Wellington
New Zealand

Dr. Hoesung Lee
Korea Energy Economics Institute
665-1, Naeson-dong
Euiwang-si, Kyunggi-du
Korea 437-082

Robert Lion
President
"Energy 21"
95, rue de Billancourt
92100 Boulogne
France

Liu Zhaodong
Minister-Counselor for Science
and Technology
Embassy
Peoples Republic of China
2300 Connecticut Avenue, NW
Washington, DC 20008

Amory B. Lovins
Director of Research and Vice
President
Rocky Mountain Institute
1739 Snowmass Creek Road
Old Snowmass, CO 81654-9199

Christopher D. Maloney
Managing Director
Unicom Corporation
One First National Plaza
34th Floor
10 South Dearborn
Chicago, IL 60603

Jan W. Mares
EOP Group
1725 Desales Street, NW
Washington, DC 20036

Kathleen A. McGinty
Chair, Council on
Environmental Quality
The White House
Washington, DC 20500

Debra Mitchell-Fox
Director, Corporate Environment,
Health & Safety Issues
Amoco Corporation
MC 2301A
200 East Randolph
Chicago, IL 60601

Nancy C. Mohn
Director, Commercial Analysis
ABB Power Plant Systems
2000 Day Hill Rd
Windsor, CT 06095-0500

Roger Naill
Vice President
The AES Corporation
1001 North 19th Street
Arlington, VA 22209

Professor Nebojsa Nakicenovic
Project Leader
Environmentally Compatible
Energy Strategies
The International Institute for
Applied Systems Analysis
Schlossplatz 1,
A-2361, Laxenburg
Austria

William A. Nitze
Assistant Administrator
Office of International Activities
Environmental Protection Agency
Mail Code 2610R
401 M Street, SW
Washington, DC 20460

Dana Orwick
Program Director Emeritus
The Aspen Institute
6004 Winnebago Road
Bethesda, MD 20816

D. Louis Peoples
Vice Chairman and Chief
  Executive Officer
Orange and Rockland Utilities, Inc.
One Blue Hill Plaza
21st Floor
Pearl River, NY 10965

John B. Phillips
Executive Director
California Energy Coalition
1540 South Coast Highway
Suite 204
Laguna Beach, CA 92651

Paul R. Portney
President & Senior Fellow
Resources for the Future
1616 P Street, NW
Washington, DC 20036

Michael Price
Chief Operating Officer
China Light & Power Co., Ltd.
147 Argyle Street, Kowloon
Hong Kong

Tony Prophet
President & CEO
Allied Signal Power Systems, Inc.
2525 West 190th Street
Torrance, CA 90504

Frank J. Puzio
Managing Partner
Coopers & Lybrand
370 17th Street
Suite 3300
Denver, CO 80202

Jim Ragland
Director, Economic Research
  Group
Saudi Aramco Services Co.
1667 K Street, NW
Suite 1200
Washington, DC 20006

Roger Rainbow
Vice President, Global Business
  Environment
Shell International Limited
Shell Centre
London SE1 7NA
United Kingdom

James E. Rogers
Vice Chairman, CEO and
  President
Cinergy Corp.
221 East Fourth Street
Atrium 30
Cincinnati, OH 45202

Bryan Sanchez
Special Assistant to the Chairman
Seven Seas Petroleum, Inc.
1990 Post Oak Boulevard
Suite 960
Houston, TX 77056

Roger W. Sant
Chairman
The AES Corporation
1001 North 19th Street
Arlington, VA 22209

Robert N. Schock
Deputy Associate Director
Lawrence Livermore National
    Laboratory
P.O. Box 808
L640
7000 East Avenue
Livermore, CA 94551

George A. Schreiber, Jr.
Executive Vice President/Chief
    Financial Officer
Arizona Public Service Company
P.O. Box 53999
Mail Station 9042
Phoenix, AZ 85072-3999

Sanford Selman
President
Selman & Co.
23 Cardinal Road
Weston, CT 06883

The Honorable Philip R. Sharp
Kennedy School of Government
Harvard University
79 John F. Kennedy Street
Cambridge, MA 02138

Robert Shaw
President
Aretê Corporation
P.O. Box 1299
Center Harbor, NH 03226

John Shlaes
JBS Associates
5505 Connecticut Avenue, NW
Washington, DC 20015

Carole B. Snyder
Senior Vice President
Corporate Affairs
GPU Services, Inc.
300 Madison Avenue
P.O. Box 1911
Morristown, NJ 07962-1911

Steven R. Spencer
Senior Vice President
External Affairs
Southern Company
270 Peachtree Street, NW
Atlanta, GA 30303

Tim D. Statton
President
Bechtel Power & Industrial
50 Beale Street
San Francisco, CA 94105

Robert N. Stavins
Professor of Public Policy and
Faculty Chair
Environment and Natural
Resources Program
Kennedy School of Government
Harvard University
79 John F. Kennedy Street
Cambridge, MA 02138

Gerald M. Stokes
Associate Laboratory Director
Battelle, Pacific Northwest
Laboratories
Environmental and Health
Sciences Division
P.O. Box 999
Richland, WA 99352

Tsutomu Toichi
Director
Institute of Energy Economics,
Japan
Shuwa Kamiyacho
Building 3-13
Toranomon
4 Chome Minato-ku
Tokyo 105, Japan

Admiral Richard H. Truly
Director
National Renewable Energy
Laboratory
1617 Cole Boulevard
Golden, CO 80401-3393

Clinton A. Vince, Esq.
Co-Chairman
Verner, Liipfert, Bernhard,
McPherson & Hand
901 15th Street, NW
Suite 700
Washington, DC 20005

Andrew W. Williams
Group Vice President
Energy, Market Policy &
Development
Potomac Electric Power Company
1900 Pennsylvania Avenue, NW
Washington, DC 20068

Mason Willrich
Chairman
Energy Works, LLC
38 Dudley Court
Piedmont, CA 94611

Ben Yamagata
Senior Partner
Van Ness, Feldman, P.C.
1050 Thomas Jefferson Street, NW
Suite 700
Washington, DC 20007

Michael Yokell
Director
Hagler, Bailly, Inc.
P.O. Drawer O
Boulder, CO 80306

Eric Zausner
President
Energy Asset Management, LLC
One Sansome Street
Suite 2100
San Francisco, CA 94104

The Aspen Institute Program on Energy, the Environment, and the Economy

The mission of **The Aspen Institute** is to enhance the quality of leadership through informed dialogue about the timeless ideas and values of the world's great cultures and traditions as they relate to the foremost challenges facing societies, organizations, and individuals. The Seminar Programs enable leaders to draw on these values to enrich their understanding of contemporary issues. The Policy Programs frame the choices that democratic societies face in terms of the enduring ideas and values derived from those traditions.

The **Program on Energy, the Environment, and the Economy** provides neutral ground for nonpartisan dialogue among diverse participants from the energy industry, government, environmental and other public interest groups, research institutions, the media, and elsewhere. Meetings in a non-adversarial setting encourage positive, candid interaction and seek areas of consensus or improved mutual understanding.

The annual **Energy Policy Forum** is the flagship of the Program. Now in its 22nd year, its high level participation, lively discussion, and congenial setting cause some of the most influential leaders in the energy sector to return again and again to grapple with timely topics facing energy policy makers. Session chairs and speakers serve only as discussion starters; participants with different perspectives contribute to and enrich the dialogue, with the goal of enhanced understanding and, where possible, consensus on policy recommendations.

The **Pacific Rim Series,** in its 16th year, consists of annual workshops for experts from industry, government, and other institutions to discuss Asian energy issues.

The **Central and Eastern European Series** begun in Prague in 1995 and continued with a Krakow meeting in 1997, convenes diverse participants from newly democratic states of the region and a few Western experts for workshops on the energy problems and opportunities.

The **Series on the Environment in the 21st Century** is a continuing dialogue among business, environmental, and government leaders about developing a new, less prescriptive, and more effective environmental protection system for the United States. In its current phase, participants are considering new ways to deal with natural resources and systems.

Valuing Environmental Performance is a dialogue among corporations and financial institutions to find ways to better communicate the strategic value of corporate environmental behavior and for financial markets to recognize and reward improvements.

A series on **Disposition and Storage of Nuclear Waste — Implications for Nonproliferation and the Environment** will allow a small number of experts and advocates from government, industry, academia, and public interest organizations to seek consensus on — and improve communication and understanding among adversaries regarding — civilian and defense nuclear waste.

A high-level **India-U.S. Electricity Restructuring Workshop** held in Jaipur, Rajasthan, in April, 1998, considered private and public ownership and regulation of power infrastructure in the two countries, including their effect on investment, consumer prices, fuel choice, and the environment.

AFTER KYOTO: ARE THERE RATIONAL PATHWAYS
TO A SUSTAINABLE GLOBAL ENERGY SYSTEM?

51

John A. Riggs is Executive Director of The Aspen Institute's Program on Energy, the Environment, and the Economy. Prior to joining the Institute he was Deputy Assistant Secretary and Acting Assistant Secretary for Policy in the U.S. Department of Energy and staff director of the Energy and Power Subcommittee of the U.S. House of Representatives. He has also taught energy and environmental policy at the University of Pennsylvania.

Susan OMalley Wade is Associate Director of the Program on Energy, the Environment, and the Economy. With specialties in natural resources management and environmental dispute resolution, she has worked as an environmental consultant in the private sector, with the California Environmental Protection Agency, and on the staff of a U.S. House of Representatives committee.